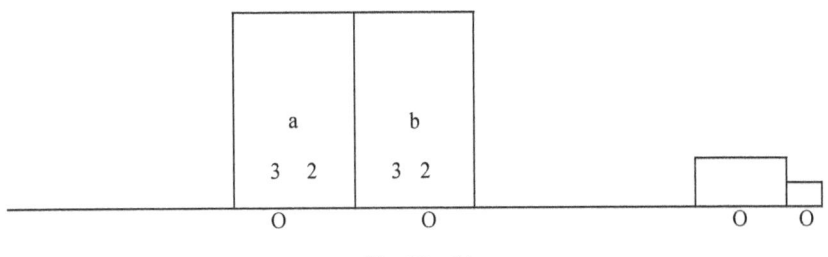

$$32 + 32 = 64$$

DYNAMIC DISTRIBUTIONS
— OF —
BINOMIALS

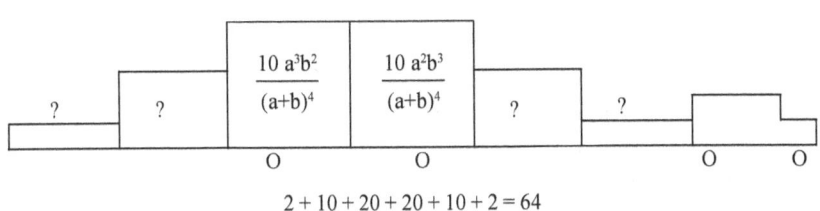

$$2 + 10 + 20 + 20 + 10 + 2 = 64$$

JOSEPH B. SALCIDO

Order this book online at www.trafford.com
or email orders@trafford.com

Most Trafford titles are also available at major online book retailers.

Printed in the United States of America.

ISBN: 978-1-4669-8908-5 (sc)
ISBN: 978-1-4669-8907-8 (e)

Trafford rev. 03/21/2014

 www.trafford.com

North America & international
toll-free: 1 888 232 4444 (USA & Canada)
fax: 812 355 4082

CONTENTS

INTRODUCTION

Binomials and foiling go hand-in-hand and are very important topics in mathematics. In this book we will investigate and rediscover these two topics.

Binomials are nouns and to foil is an infinitive. To foil a binomial is an algebraic operation, called and done to remove ( )'s: $(a+b)^2 = a^2 + 2ab + b^2$. Notice three terms are the result. We'll discuss and execute the steps on the removal of ( )'s.

The first time, that I remember hearing the word 'binomial', I cannot recall. I believe it must have been around 1960. I don't recollect dates, though, I do remember Mr. Danny Kinnard, my high school Math teacher, at Miami H.S. in Ariz, telling our class of 1965, "When $(a+b)^2$ is expanded the result is $a^2 + 2ab + b^2$. There's always one more term (3) than the index of the binomial (2)". Then he wrote on the blackboard $(a+b)^3 = a^3 + 3a^2b + 3ab^2 + b^3$, and said "one more term than index".

The reason, I can remember all this, is that those two statements stayed with me throughout my life. At times, I wondered why those two statements were true.

We learned how to expand polynomials, like every other high school math student. We learned stack multiplications:

$$\begin{array}{r} a+b \\ \times\ a+b \\ \hline a^2+ab \\ +ab+b^2 \\ \hline a^2+2ab+b^2 \end{array}$$

I believe everyone in algebra could do this operation.

Then, we learned how to foil horizontally: $(a+b)^2 = (a+b)(a+b)$ remember that one?

Then, we learned about $(a+b)^n = a^n + na^{n-1}b + \dfrac{n(n-1)a^{n-2}b^2}{2!} + ...,$ the Binomial Theorem.

All these expansions take time and memorizations, esp. the Binomial Theorem Expansion.

But all of them work for sure.

When, I was in my teens, I wondered if there were other ways to learn expansions without all the rules. All of us had a difficult time. I guess all kids are the same. The horizontal foil was and still is the easiest and fastest way to expand a simple binomial. The difficulty comes when binomials' indices are larger than three. Imagine $(a+b)^{10}$ or $(a+b)^{20}$. One would have to almost resort to stacked or the Binomial theorem of Expansion.

Well, not much was done to make binomial expansions easier by me or anyone else that I know of since that time. Kids are still doing the same manipulations.

Here we go, here's the effort I made later, because I had time, I was retired and taking care of my father-in-law Juan.

I retired in 2003. I really believe, if I wasn't taking care of Juan, I wouldn't have discovered the 'Salcido's Vertical Foil'. Thank you Juan. A few months before Juan died in 2007, we were watching a TV program together. I started dozing-off when a thought struck me, why not foil vertically?

I immediately thought nobody has thought of this. Let's try it, maybe it'll work. But, in my mind, I couldn't and didn't know where and how to start. I tried different formats, but the one I liked the best is in this book. I'll show you how it all happened, one event after another.

I will, also, tell you about binomial's close 'but foreign to us' cousin, Nanomial. A Nanomial has terms when expanded just like binomials have, but in a different way. The terms of a Nanomial are called nanos. Nanomial's quite an interesting relative. I don't know what gender Nanomial is, so we'll say it's an it. It can be very obliging if you don't get under it's ( )'s. Nanomial is a controlling character and it's domain is the real number world. Nanomial doesn't care about strict rules, like, one more term than exponent jargon. Nanomial will use however or how many exponents and terms it needs to complete the job!

In this book you'll learn who Nanomial is and how it reacts to situations you present to it. Using 'Salcido's Vertical Nanomial Foil' will be very interesting and challenging.

Nanomial has its own family tree, whom you'll meet.

Seriously, there are three main ideas in this book:

1) Salcido's Vertical Foil
2) Salcido's Nanomial Theorem
3) Salcido's Nanomial Vertical Foil

The three ideas above result in Nanoization.

I don't know how these three ideas are going to be accepted, because, I'm neither a professional Mathematician, or PHD, only a professional wonderer.

So from the proverbial "Shoulders of giants", this is my contribution to whomever appreciates Nanomial and it's Nanos, hope the giants approve!

Enjoy the Book

Joseph B. Salcido
2012

CHAPTER I

What are binomials? A binomial is a quantity sum of two terms: (a+b), $(2+3)^4$, $(1+x)^2$, etc. To expand these binomials means to remove the ( )'s.

First, we recall, any factor raised to the zero index or power is equal to one (1), ie - $(x+y)^0 = 1$, next, any factor raised to the exponent, index, power all meaning the same (1), ie $(x+y)^1$ or (x+y) = x+y, $(7+3)^1 = 7+3$. Let's try some examples $7^0=1$, $(7+0)^1 = 7+0$, $(w-y)^0 = 1$, $(w-y)^1$ or (w-y) = w-y, $(n-1)^0 = 1$, on and on.

Moving on, with a quantity binomial raised to some index or power: $(a+b)^n$. Let n=2, then $(a+b)^2$ may be expanded by stacked multiplication:

$$
\begin{array}{r}
a + b \\
a + b \\
\hline
a^2 + ab \\
+ ab + b^2 \\
\hline
a^2 + 2ab + b^2
\end{array}
$$

This is a process we learned in H.S. algebra.

Another is : Horizontal Foil

$$(a+b)^2 = (a+b)(a+b)$$

1

the other is: Binomial theorem $\exp.(a+b)^n = \left[a\left(1+\dfrac{b}{a}\right)\right]^n$

or $(a+b)^n = a^n + na^{n-1}b + \dfrac{n(n-1)a^{n-2}}{2!}b^2 + \ldots$

Now let's try something NEW!

'SALCIDO'S VERTICAL FOIL' Table

Foil	Terms	Term #
$1 \times 2 \div 1 = 2$	$1\ a^2\ b^0$	1
$2 \times 1 \div 2 = 1$	$2\ a^1\ b^1$	2
	$1\ a^0\ b^2$	3

Notice the index of $(a+b)^2$ is 2.

which, also tells us there are three terms in the expansion.

Here's how you do it. Set up the basic 'Salcido's Vertical Foil' Table (later on other label headings may be added:

Foil	Terms	Term #

then: Fill in the *term* # Col.

Foil	Terms	*Term #*
		1
		2
		3

then: Fill in the Terms col.

Foil	Terms	Term #
$1 \times 2 \div 1 = 2$	$1\ a^2\ b^0$	1
$2 \times 1 \div 2 = 1$	$2\ a^1\ b^1$	2
	$1\ a^0\ b^2$	3

$$a^2 + 2ab + b^2$$

Then do the foil operations under the foil column.

Let's try: $(a+b)^4$

Foil	Terms	Term #
$1 \times 4 \div 1 = 4$	$1\ a^4\ b^0$	1
$4 \times 3 \div 2 = 6$	$4\ a^3\ b^1$	2
$6 \times 2 \div 3 = 4$	$6\ a^2\ b^2$	3
$4 \times 1 \div 4 = 1$	$4\ a^1\ b^3$	4
	$1\ a^0\ b^4$	5

$$a^4 + 4a^3b + 6a^2b^2 + 4ab^3 + b^4$$

A little more difficult one:

$$(a+b)^{10}$$

Foil	Terms	Term #
$1 \times 10 \div 1 = 10$	$1\ a^{10}\ b^0$	1
$10 \times 9 \div 2 = 45$	$10\ a^9\ b^1$	2
$45 \times 8 \div 3 = 120$	$45\ a^8\ b^2$	3
$120 \times 7 \div 4 = 210$	$120\ a^7\ b^3$	4
$210 \times 6 \div 5 = 252$	$210\ a^6\ b^4$	5
$252 \times 5 \div 6 = 210$	$252\ a^5\ b^5$	6
$210 \times 4 \div 7 = 120$	$210\ a^4\ b^6$	7
$120 \times 3 \div 8 = 45$	$120\ a^3\ b^7$	8
$45 \times 2 \div 9 = 10$	$45\ a^2\ b^8$	9
$10 \times 1 \div 10 = 1$	$10\ a^1\ b^9$	10
	$1\ a^0\ b^{10}$	11

$$a^{10} + 10\ a^9b + 45\ a^8b^2 + 120\ a^7b^3 + 210\ a^6b^4$$
$$+252\ a^5b^5 + 210\ a^4b^6 + 120\ a^3b^7$$
$$+45\ a^2b^8 + 10\ ab^9 + b^{10}$$

So, with the 'Salcido's Vertical Foil' expanding $(a+b)^n$, where n is a counting number, becomes very easy compared to those other methods. How about $(a+b)^{50}$! with a hand held calculator this is a very easy accomplishment!

Here's, also, an easy way to find a certain term w/ its coefficient and exponent.

consider: $(a+b)^{50}$; find its 10th term.

1) Set up literal factors w/ exponents:

$$\frac{50 \cdot 49 \cdot 48 \cdot 47 \cdot 46 \cdot 45 \cdot 44 \cdot 43 \cdot 42}{9 \cdot 8 \cdot 7 \cdot 6 \cdot 5 \cdot 4 \cdot 3 \cdot 2 \cdot 1} \qquad a^{41}b^9$$

$$50 \cdot 49 \cdot 47 \cdot 46 \cdot 11 \cdot 43 \qquad a^{41}b^9$$

Study this, look at no. of factors in the denominator and numerator (exponent of b).

Let's see: $(a+b)^7$, find 4th term

$$\frac{7 \cdot 6 \cdot 5}{3 \cdot 2 \cdot 1} \quad a^4 b^3$$

$$35\ a^4\ b^3$$

Be investigative, by that I mean, why did this or that happen? Why was that the result? This is what the book's all about: comparing, separating, analyzing, collections and then re-doing these four steps as necessary 'til the expected result is achieved.

We will revisit this chapter. In the next chapter Nanoization will be completely scrutinized. Here's an example:

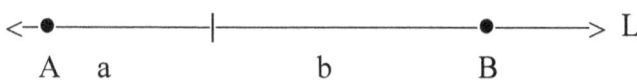

$$\begin{array}{cccc} \text{A} & \text{a} & \text{b} & \text{B} \end{array} \qquad \text{L}$$

In this book 'a' and 'b', '$(a+b)^n$' will be used consistently in order to keep operations as simple as possible.

Let's Nanoize the segment $\overline{AB}$ from 2 segments to 6 segments

$$a+b = S_1 + S_2 + S_3 + S_4 + S_5 + S_6$$

Nanoize $(a+b)^1$, $(a+b)^2$, $(a+b)^{10}$, $(a+b)^3$ etc will become commonplace subjects of interest.

CHAPTER II

Nanomial

How is the best way to introduce a complete stranger to someone? A best foot forward would do.

I would like you to meet Nanomial. It likes to do the *same things* cousin 'Binomial' does follows all the algebraic rules, laws, theories of computations, goes through expansions the same way, and is very obliging to geometrical formations and representations.

How Nanomial is different from Binomial is that it has a denominator in each of it's terms, when expanded; in this paradigm, its terms are called Nanos. Each Nano of the expansion has the same denominator.

In order to find out exactly what a Nanomial is, and how it's brought about is next.

Time for:

'SALCIDO'S NANOMIAL THEOREM'

$$(a+b)^n = (a+b)^{m-1}/(a+b)^{m-n-1}$$

The best way to illustrate this theorem is to give m and n values, any real numbers will do: $n = 3$, $m = 8$

1) $(a+b)^3 = (a+b)^7/(a+b)^4$

Now: expand the numerator use: 'SALCIDO'S Vertical Foil' Table

Foil	Terms	Term #	Value
$1 \times 7 \div 1 = 7$	$a^7/(a+b)^4$	1	.2048
$7 \times 6 \div 2 = 21$	$7\,a^6\,b/(a+b)^4$	2	2.1504
$21 \times 5 \div 3 = 35$	$21\,a^5\,b^2/(a+b)^4$	3	9.6768
$35 \times 4 \div 4 = 35$	$35\,a^4\,b^3/(a+b)^4$	4	24.192
$35 \times 3 \div 5 = 21$	$35\,a^3\,b^4/(a+b)^4$	5	36.288
$21 \times 2 \div 6 = 7$	$21\,a^2\,b^5/(a+b)^4$	6	32.6592
$7 \times 1 \div 7 = 1$	$7\,a\,b^6/(a+b)^4$	7	16.3296
	$1\,b^7/(a+b)^4$	8	+ 3.4992
			125

How do we check:

Let: $a = 2$, $b = 3$
   (or any other Nos)
$(a+b)^n = (2+3)^3 = 125$

So, as you can see $(a+b)^3$ has 8 terms!!

$(a+b)^3$ may have any number of terms that's required of it.

2) $(a+b)^3 \rightarrow 12$ terms

$$(a+b)^3 = (a+b)^{11}/(a+b)^8$$

Foil	Terms	Term #	Value
$1 \times 11 \div 11 = 11$	$1\ a^{11}\ b^0/(a+b)^8$	1	8.470045193
$11 \times 10 \div 2 = 55$	$11\ a^{10}\ b^1/(a+b)^8$	2	37.26819885
$55 \times 9 \div 3 = 165$	$55\ a^9\ b^2/(a+b)^8$	3	74.5363977
$165 \times 8 \div 4 = 330$	$165\ a^8\ b^3/(a+b)^8$	4	89.44367724
$330 \times 7 \div 5 = 462$	$330\ a^7\ b^4/(a+b)^8$	5	71.55494179
$462 \times 6 \div 6 = 462$	$462\ a^6\ b^5/(a+b)^8$	6	40.0707674
$462 \times 5 \div 7 = 330$	$462\ a^5\ b^6/(a+b)^8$	7	16.02830696
$330 \times 4 \div 8 = 165$	$330\ a^4\ b^7/(a+b)^8$	8	4.579516275
$165 \times 3 \div 9 = 55$	$165\ a^3\ b^8/(a+b)^8$	9	.9159032549
$55 \times 2 \div 10 = 11$	$55\ a^2\ b^9/(a+b)^8$	10	.122120434
$11 \times 1 \div 11 = 1$	$11\ a^1\ b^{10}/(a+b)^8$	11	.0097696347
	$1\ a^0\ b^{11}/(a+b)^8$	12	.0003552594443
			343

To check - Let: a = 5, b = 2

$(a+b)^n = (5+2)^3$
$\qquad = 343$

3) $(a+b)^3 \rightarrow 6\ \text{terms} \rightarrow (a+b)^3 = \dfrac{(a+b)^5}{(a+b)^{4.7}}$

Foil	Terms	Term #	Value
if you have to use the foil col.	$a^5/(a+b)^{4.7}$	1	.0068467757
use it.	$5\,a^4\,b/(a+b)^{4.7}$	2	.0753145331
	$10\,a^3\,b^2/(a+b)^{4.7}$	3	.3313839458
	$10\,a^2\,b^3/(a+b)^{4.7}$	4	.7290446808
	$5\,a\,b^4/(a+b)^{4.7}$	5	.8019491489
	$b^5/(a+b)^{4.7}$	6	+ .3528576255
			2.29739671

use calculator: let a = 5, b = 11

$$(a+b)^{.3} = (5+11)^{.3} = 2.29739671$$

4) $(a+b)^{-\sqrt{\pi}} \rightarrow 4$ terms

$$(a+b)^{-\sqrt{\pi}} = (a+b)^3 / (a+b)^{3+\sqrt{\pi}}$$

Terms	Term #	Value
$a^3 / (a+b)^{3+\sqrt{\pi}}$	1	.001322539
$3a^2b / (a+b)^{3+\sqrt{\pi}}$	2	.0066126949

10

$3ab^2 / (a+b)^{3+\sqrt{\pi}}$ 3   .0110211581

$b^3 / (a+b)^{3+\sqrt{\pi}}$ 4 $+ .0061228656$

                                        $\overline{}$

                                              .0250792576

check - let: a = 3, b = 5

use: calculator

$$(a+b)^n = (3+5)^{-\sqrt{\pi}} = 1/(8 \wedge (\pi \wedge .5))$$

$$= .0250792575$$

With the knowledge of chapters I & II much may be accomplished as you will see soon.

In Chapter III, we will learn how to complete vertical tables with minimal information.

CHAPTER III

Binomial expansions that are incomplete may be solved for: a^6b^7. We may start with setting-up blank terms separated with plus or minus signs, ie:

$$a^{13} + a^{12}b + a^{11}b^2 + a^{10}b^3 + a^9b^4 + a^8b^5 +$$

$$a^7b^6 + a^6b^7 + a^5b^8 + a^4b^9$$
$$+ a^3b^{10} + a^2b^{11} + ab^{12} + b^{13}$$

the above expansion results from $(a+b)^{13}$.

then: find each term's coefficient independently: the 8th term of $(a+b)^{13}$ is -

$$\frac{13 \cdot 12 \cdot 11 \cdot 10 \cdot 9 \cdot 8 \cdot 7}{7 \cdot 6 \cdot 5 \cdot 4 \cdot 3 \cdot 2} \quad a^6b^7 = 1716a^6b^7$$

In similar fashion the other 13 coefficients may be solved for. OR, $(a+b)^{13}$ may be expanded.

Let's try 'Vertical Foil'

An example related to the following few pages.

Given: A binomial train of four cars: $(a+b)^3$

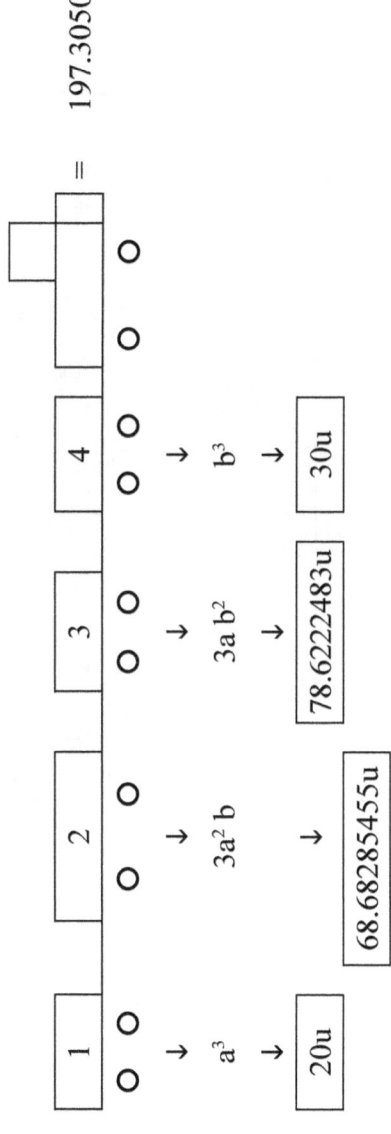

given: $a = 20^{1/3}$, $b = 30^{1/3}$

convert: To a Nanomial Train of Ten cars - $(a+b)^9/(a+b)^6$

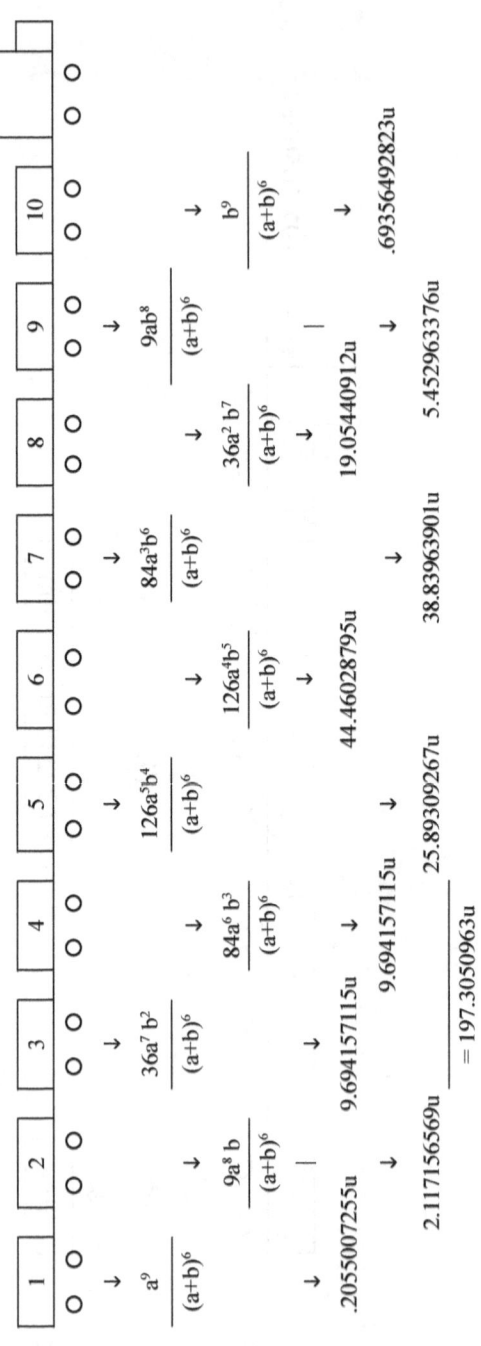

$$\frac{a^9}{(a+b)^6} \quad \frac{9a^8 b}{(a+b)^6} \quad \frac{36a^7 b^2}{(a+b)^6} \quad \frac{84a^6 b^3}{(a+b)^6} \quad \frac{126a^5 b^4}{(a+b)^6} \quad \frac{126a^4 b^5}{(a+b)^6} \quad \frac{84a^3 b^6}{(a+b)^6} \quad \frac{36a^2 b^7}{(a+b)^6} \quad \frac{9ab^8}{(a+b)^6} \quad \frac{b^9}{(a+b)^6}$$

.2055007255u 2.117156569u 9.694157115u 9.694157115u 25.89309267u 44.46028795u 38.83963901u 19.05440912u 5.452963376u .69356492823u

= 197.3050963u

First: set-up Table

Foil	Terms		Term #
$1 \times 13 \div 1 = 13$	$1\, a^{13}$		1
$13 \times 12 \div 2 = 78$	$13\, a^{12}\, b$		2
$78 \times 11 \div 3 = 286$	$78\, a^{11}\, b^{2}$		3
$286 \times 10 \div 4 = 715$	$286\, a^{10}\, b^{3}$		4
$715 \times 9 \div 5 = 1287$	$715\, a^{9}\, b^{4}$		5
$1287 \times 8 \div 6 = 1716$	$1287\, a^{8}\, b^{5}$		6
$1716 \times 7 \div 7 = 1716$	$1716\, a^{7}\, b^{6}$		7
$1716 \times 6 \div 8 = 1287$	$1716\, a^{6}\, b^{7}$	given	8
$1287 \times 5 \div 9 = 715$	$1287\, a^{5}\, b^{8}$		9
$715 \times 4 \div 10 = 286$	$715\, a^{4}\, b^{9}$		10
$286 \times 3 \div 11 = 78$	$286\, a^{3}\, b^{10}$		11
$78 \times 2 \div 12 = 13$	$78\, a^{2}\, b^{11}$		12
$13 \times 1 \div 13 = 1$	$13\, a\, b^{12}$		13
	$1\, b^{13}$		14

Second: start at top of Term # column and put numbers as shown.

Third: Fill in ab's and corresponding exponents.

Fourth: Foil as shown.

This method is as simple as possible!

There is no, $\quad \left(\dfrac{n}{o} \right) = \dfrac{n!}{K!(n-K)!} \;$;

it's necessary to learn these methods, but once you learn them, move on to an easier method.

Nanomial expansion may be done similarly. The only difference is the denominator. Don't forget the denominator.

given: $?a^6b^7/(a+b)^4$

Foil	Terms	Term #	Value
$1 \times 13 \div 1 = 13$	$1\ a^{13}/(a+b)^4$	1	
	$13\ a^{12}\ b/(a+b)^4$	2	
		3	
		4	
		5	
		6	
		7	
given	$?\ a^6\ b^7/(a+b)^4$	8	
		9	
		10	
		11	
		12	
		13	
		14	

The coefficients are the same for this table as in the previous table. The denominator makes it a 'Nano Vertical' Table.
-Note-

$(a+b)^9$ is expanded to 14 terms, not 10 terms.

Notice in the value column there are no entries, that's because a and b don't have any numerical values.

Let's go back to $(a+b)^3$, where a=2, b=4 for an easy example. Set-up table

Foil	Terms	Term #	Value
use this column if needed.	a^3	1	8
	$3\,a^2\,b$	2	48
	$3\,a\,b^2$	3	96
	b^3	4	+ 64
			216

$(a+b)^3 = (2+4)^3 = 6^3 = 216$

Now let's try the Nanonial expansion of $(a+b)^3$ to 6 terms, where a = 2, b = 4. (use: Salcido's Nanomial theorem)

Foil	Terms	Term #	Value
	$a^5/(a+b)^2$	1	$.\overline{8}$
	$5\,a^4\,b/(a+b)^2$	2	$8.\overline{8}$
	$10\,a^3\,b^2/(a+b)^2$	3	$35.\overline{5}$
	$10\,a^2\,b^3/(a+b)^2$	4	$71.\overline{1}$
To check:	$5\,a\,b^4/(a+b)^2$	5	$71.\overline{1}$
	$b^5/(a+b)^2$	6	$+ 28.\overline{4}$

To check: $(a+b)^3 = (2+4)^3 = 216$ 216

Being able to fill in these 'tables', we can move on to solving for term's value for each term by only knowing the values of two terms, no matter the Size of Tables.

For instance: Given table

Foil	Terms	Term #		Value below:
	a^5	1	given	.5
	$5\,a^4\,b$	2	given	1.0
	$10\,a^3\,b^2$	3	?	.8
	$10\,a^2\,b^3$	4	?	.32
	$5\,a\,b^4$	5	?	.064
	b^5	6	?	+ .00512
				2.68912

Solution:

given: $a^5 = .5$, $5\,a^4\,b = 1.0$
    $a = .5^{.2}$, substitute $.5^{.2}$ for 'a'
into Term # 2 equation.

$5(.5^{.2})^4\,b = 1$
$b = 1/5(.5^{.2})^4$

$b = .3482202253$
$a = .8705505633$

To check:

$(a+b)^5 = (.8705505633 + .3482202253)^5$
$= 2.68912$

18

Related to next few pages.

$$a^9 + 9\,a^8b + \ldots + b^9 \rightarrow \text{ten terms}$$
$$\downarrow \qquad\qquad \downarrow$$
$$4 \qquad\qquad 7$$

then: $a = 4^{1/9}$ then: $b = 7^{1/9}$

Change $(a+b)^9 \rightarrow 10$ terms to $(a+b)^9 \rightarrow$ two terms

$(a+b)^9 = (a+b)/(a+b)^{-8} \rightarrow$ Two Terms

$= a(a+b)^8 + b(a+b)^8$

$= 4^{1/9}(4^{1/9} + 7^{1/9})^8 + 7^{1/9}(4^{1/9} + 7^{1/9})^8$

Two Terms $\rightarrow$ $1318.243708 + 1402.813493$
            $=$ 2721.057201

check:

Ten Terms $\rightarrow$

a^9	4
$9\,a^8\,b$	38.30952158
$36\,a^7\,b^2$	163.0688271
$84\,a^6\,b^3$	404.9039004
$126\,a^5\,b^4$	646.3197795
$126\,a^4\,b^5$	687.7833761
$84\,a^3\,b^6$	487.9380016
$36\,a^2\,b^7$	222.5318024
$9\,a\,b^8$	59.20199226
b^9	7
	2721.057201

another one:

Foil	Terms	Term #		Value
	?	1	?	
	?	2	?	
	? $a^?$ $b^?$	3		$.\overline{7}$
	?	4	?	
	? $a^?$ $b^?$	5	?	
		6	?	
		7	?	
	? $a^?$ $b^?$	8		.4321
	?	9	?	
	?	10	?	

See if you can do this one?

$(a+b)^?$, Fill in Table, and check work w/ a = 3, b = 5.

Solution.

Foil	Terms	Term #	Value
	a^9	1	.0273313784
	$9\,a^8\,b$	2	.2187005079
given	$36\,a^7\,b^2$	3	$.\overline{7}$
	$84\,a^6\,b^3$	4	1.613533783
	$126\,a^5\,b^4$	5	2.151865234
	$126\,a^4\,b^5$	6	1.913201957
	$84\,a^3\,b^6$	7	1.134005875

20

given $\quad$ $36\,a^2\,b^7$ $\qquad$ 8 $\qquad$ .4321

$\qquad\qquad\quad$ $9\,a\,b^8$ $\qquad$ 9 $\qquad$ .0960439521

$\qquad\qquad\qquad$ b^9 $\qquad$ 10 $\qquad$ + .0094879691

$\qquad\qquad\qquad\qquad\qquad$ Check: $\quad$ 8.374048433

$$36\,a^7\,b^2 = \overline{7}\,;\ 36a^2b^7 = .4321$$

$$36 = \frac{\overline{7}}{a^7b^2}\,, \qquad\qquad 36 = \frac{.4321}{a^2b^7}$$

$$\frac{\overline{7}}{a^7b^2} = \frac{.4321}{a^2b^7}$$

$$\frac{\overline{7}}{a^5} = \frac{.4321}{b^5}$$

$$\frac{a^5}{\overline{7}} = \frac{b^5}{.4321}$$

$$a^5 = \frac{\overline{7}\left(b^5\right)}{.4321}$$

$$a = \left[\frac{\overline{7}\left(b^5\right)}{.4321}\right]^{.2}$$

$$a = 1.12474547b$$

Substitute $1.12474547b$ for 'a'

in Term #3:

$$36 \, (1.12474547b)^7 \, b^2 = .\overline{7}$$

$$36(1.12474547)^7 \, b^9 = .\overline{7}$$

$$b = \left[\frac{.\overline{7}}{36(1.12474547)^7} \right]^{1/9}$$

$$b = .5959934315$$

$$a = .6703409123$$

check:

$$(a+b)^9 = (.6703409123 + .5959934315)^9$$

$$= 8.374048432$$

Now a Nano Table
Fill in the table

Foil	Terms	Term #		Value
	$a^4/(a+b)^2$	1	Given	.4
	$4 \, a^3 \, b/(a+b)^2$	2	?	1.770691073
	$6 \, a^2 \, b^2/(a+b)^2$	3	?	2.939387695
	$4 \, a \, b^3/(a+b)^2$	4	?	2.168644812
	$b^4/(a+b)^2$	5	Given	.6
			check:	7.878723581

$a^4/(a+b)^2 = .4;$ $\qquad b^4/(a+b)^2 = .6$

$$(a+b)^2 = \frac{a^4}{.4} \; ; \; (a+b)^2 = \frac{b^4}{.6}$$

$$\frac{a^4}{.4} = \frac{b^4}{.6}$$

$$\frac{a}{.4^{.25}} = \frac{b}{.6^{.25}}$$

$$a = \frac{.4^{.25}b}{.6^{.25}}$$

$a = .9036020036b$

Substitute .9036020036b for 'a' into Term # 1.

$(.9036020036b)^4/(.9036020036b + b)^2 = .4$

$$\frac{(.9036020036b)^4}{(.9036020036b + b)^2} = .4$$

$$\frac{.9036020036^4 b^4}{b^2(1.9036020036)^2} = .4$$

$b = 1.474523772$

$a = 1.332382634$

check:

$$(a+b)^2 = (1.474523772 + 1.332382634)^2$$

$$= 7.878723572$$

Another example:

Given: $(a+b)^{1.7} \rightarrow 8$ Terms; 2nd Term = 2; 6th Term = 4

Find: Value of $(a+b)^{1.7}$; set up Nanomial Vertical Foil Table with Columns - Foil, Terms, Term #, Value; Fill in all columns; Use 'Salcido's Nanomial Theorem'.

Solution next page.

Given: expand $(a+b)^{1.7} \rightarrow$ 8 terms

$(a+b)^{1.7} = (a+b)^{7}/(a+b)^{5.3}$

Foil	Terms	Term #		Value
	$a^{7}/(a+b)^{5.3}$	1		.3161948415
	$7\,a^{6}\,b/(a+b)^{5.3}$	2	Given	2
	$21\,a^{5}b^{2}/(a+b)^{5.3}$	3		5.421612085
	$35\,a^{4}\,b^{3}/(a+b)^{5.3}$	4		8.164965859
	$35\,a^{3}\,b^{4}/(a+b)^{5.3}$	5		7.377879468
	$21\,a^{2}\,b^{5}/(a+b)^{5.3}$	6	Given	4
	$7\,a\,b^{6}/(a+b)^{5.3}$	7		1.204802658
	$b^{7}/(a+b)^{5.3}$	8		+ .1555231557
			check:	28.64097807

$7\,a^{6}\,b/(a+b)^{5.3} = 2,\ 21\,a^{2}\,b^{5}/(a+b)^{5.3} = 4$

$14\,a^{6}\,b/(a+b)^{5.3} = 4,$ "

$14\,a^{6}\,b/4 = (a+b)^{5.3},\ 21\,a^{2}\,b^{5}/4 = (a+b)^{5.3}$

$$\frac{14a^{6}b}{4} = \frac{21a^{2}b^{5}}{4}$$

$2\,a^{4} = 3\,b^{4}$

$a = (1.5)^{.25}\,b$

$a = 1.10668192b$

Substitute 1.0668192b for 'a' in term #2:

$$\frac{7(1.10668192b)^6\, b}{(1.10668192b + b)^{5.3}} = 2$$

$$\frac{7(1.10668192)^6\, b^7}{b^{5.3}(2.10668192)^{5.3}} = 2$$

$$b^{1.7} = 8.069926832$$

$$b = 3.415487531$$

$$a = 3.779858319$$

check:

$$(a+b)^{1.7} = (3.779858319 + 3.415487531)^{1.7}$$

$$= 28.64097808$$

CHAPTER IV

1) A line segment: S

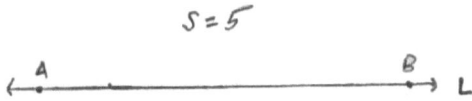

may be parted into 2 or more pieces:

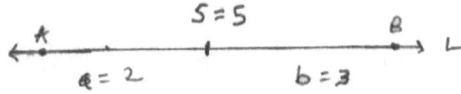

A piece or pieces may have predetermined lengths.

For example, let a = 2 and b = 3, but how about S_1 through S_9? We may predetermine the segments S_1 through S_9. S_1 = .1, S_2 = .4, S_3 = 2, S_4 = .01, S_5 = .07, S_6 = 1, S_7 = 1.1, S_8 = .3, S_9 = .02 by painfully adding and subtracting, until all pieces equal 5.

Why not choose a binomial to do the work for you, unless those are the exact segments that are needed?

Maybe, for a design, why not let a binomial do the work? It's, also, easy to change the values of 'a' & 'b'.

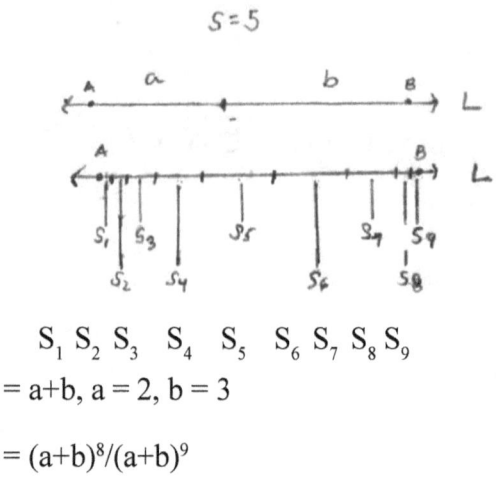

$$S = 5$$

$$S_1 \; S_2 \; S_3 \; S_4 \; S_5 \; S_6 \; S_7 \; S_8 \; S_9$$

$$S = a+b, \; a = 2, \; b = 3$$

$$S = (a+b)^8/(a+b)^9$$

Recognize 'Salcido's Nanomial Theorem'?

Side	Terms	Term #	Value
S_1	$a^8/(a+b)^7$	1	.0032768
S_2	$8 \, a^7 \, b/(a+b)^7$	2	.0393216
S_3	$28 \, a^6 \, b^2/(a+b)^7$	3	.2064384
S_4	$56 \, a^5 \, b^3/(a+b)^7$	4	.6193915
S_5	$70 \, a^4 \, b^4/(a+b)^7$	5	1.161216
S_6	$56 \, a^3 \, b^5/(a+b)^7$	6	1.3934592
S_7	$28 \, a^2 \, b^6/(a+b)^7$	7	1.0450944
S_8	$8 \, a \, b^7/(a+b)^7$	8	.4478976
S_9	$b^8/(a+b)^7$	9	+ .0839808
$S =$			5.0000763

There may be an argument as to "what good is this type of knowledge? All I can say is "What good is $y = x^2$, $\ln x$? They are only math relationships. The way they are applied is of value".

2) A Square: y

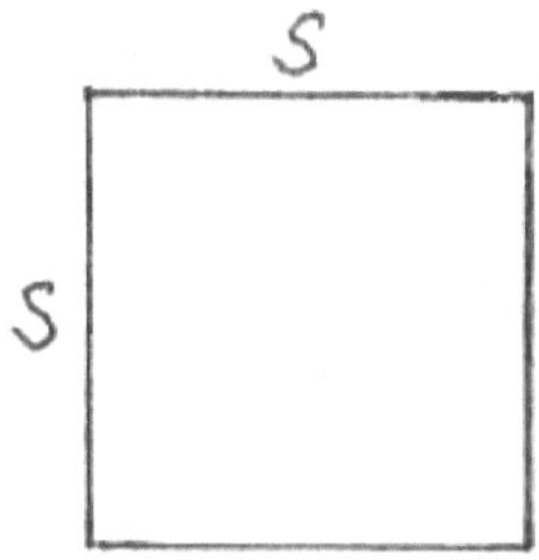

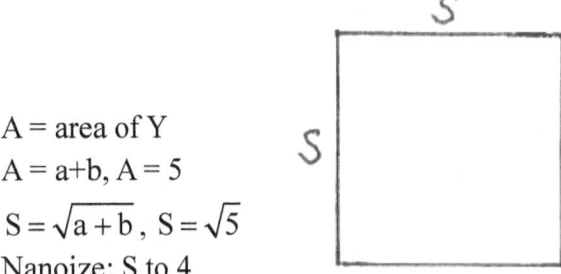

A = area of Y

A = a+b, A = 5

$S = \sqrt{a+b}$, $S = \sqrt{5}$

Nanoize: S to 4

'S' may be parted into 2 or more pieces:

$\sqrt{a+b}$

$\sqrt{a+b}$		S_1	S_2	S_3	S_4
	S_1	A_1			
	S_2	A_2			
	S_3	A_3			
	S_4	A_4			A_{16}

A piece or pieces may have predetermined lengths and/or areas. Again, we may randomly choose values for S_1 through S_4 that add to $\sqrt{5}$. But, Nanomial comes to the rescue.

A = a+b, A = S^2, S = $(a+b)^{1/2}$

* remember to check: letting, a = 2, b = 3

S = $(a+b)^{1/2} = (a+b)^3/(a+b)^{2.5}$

Now: Substitute for 'a' and 'b' in the table.

Side	Terms	Term #	Value
S_1	$a^3/(a+b)^{2.5}$	1	.1431083506
S_2	$3\ a^2\ b/(a+b)^{2.5}$	2	.643975775
S_3	$3\ a\ b^2/(a+b)^{2.5}$	3	.9659813663
S_4	$b^3/(a+b)^{2.5}$	4	+ .4829906831
S =			2.23605615

check: $S = \sqrt{5} = 2.236067977$

$A_1 = S_1^2 = .02048$ $A_9 = S_3 \cdot S_1 = .13824$

$A_2 = S_1 \cdot S_2 = .092158311$ $A_{10} = S_3 \cdot S_2 = .622068599$

$A_3 = S_1 \cdot S_3 = .13824$ $A_{11} = S_3^2 = .93312$

$A_4 = S_1 \cdot S_4 = .06912$ $A_{12} = S_3 \cdot S_4 = .46656$

$A_5 = S_2 \cdot S_1 = .092158311$ $A_{13} = S_4 \cdot S_1 = .06912$

$A6 = S_2^2 = .4147047988$ $A_{14} = S_4 \cdot S_2 = .3110342995$

$A_7 = S_2 \cdot S_3 = .622068599$ $A_{15} = S_4 \cdot S_3 = .46656$

$A8 = S_2 \cdot S_4 = .3110342995$ $A_{16} = S_4^2 = .23328$

$A = $ 5.0

3) A cube: c

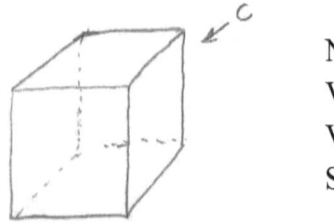

Nanoize S to 7

$V = a+b, \ V = 5$

$V = S^3, \ S = V^{1/3}$

$S = (a+b)^{1/3} = 5^{1/3}$

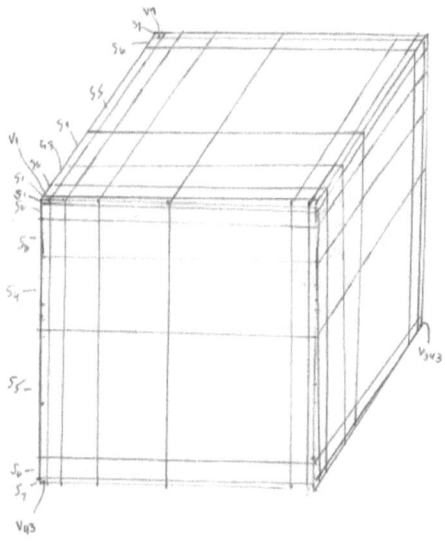

$$S = (a+b)^{\frac{1}{3}} = (a+b)^6/(a+b)^{17/3}$$

$$S = S_1 + S_2 + S_3 + S_4 + S_5 + S_6 + S_7$$

There are 343 rectangular solids in C. Predetermined sides and volumes of the smaller solids are obtained and recorded to show the ability of this process.

$$(a+b)^{\frac{1}{2}} = (a+b)^6/(a+b)^{17/3}$$

Side	Terms	Term #	Value
S_1	$a^6/(a+b)^{17/3}$	1	.0070040615
S_2	$6a^5b/(a+b)^{17/3}$	2	.0630365533
S_3	$15\,a^4\,b^2/(a+b)^{17/3}$	3	.2363870749

31

S4	$20\ a^3\ b^3/(a+b)^{17/3}$	4	.4727741497
S_5	$15\ a^2\ b^4/(a+b)^{17/3}$	5	.5318709185
S_6	$6\ a\ b^5/(a+b)^{17/3}$	6	.3191225511
$\underline{S_7}$	$b^6/(a+b)^{17/3}$	7	$\underline{+ .0797806378}$
$S =$			1.709975947

check:

$$S = (5)^{1/3} = 1.709975947$$

$V_1 = S_1^{\ 3} = .000000343597387$ (smallest)
$V_2 = S_1^{\ 2} \cdot S_2 = ?$

$V_3 = S_1^{\ 2} \cdot S_3 = ?$ there are too many (343 solids)
$V_4 = S_1^{\ 2} \cdot S_4 = ?$ to figure, but the idea is, it's possible.
$V_5 = S_1^{\ 2} \cdot S_5 = ?$
$V_6 = S_1^{\ 2} \cdot S_6 = ?$
$V_7 = S_1^{\ 2} \cdot S_7 = ?$, $V_{239} = .1504591951$ (Largest)

V_{239} is 437,893.8863 times

Larger than V_1!

4) A plane circle: W

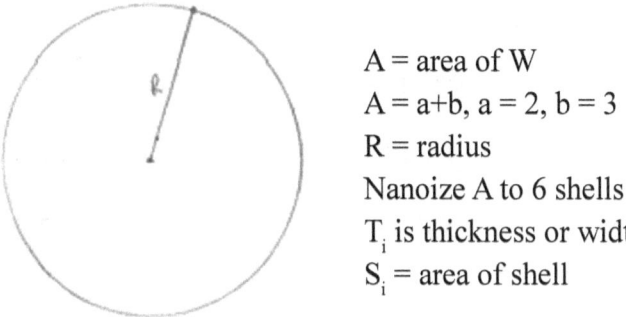

A = area of W
A = a+b, a = 2, b = 3
R = radius
Nanoize A to 6 shells
T_i is thickness or width
S_i = area of shell

Circle W may be parted in to shell areas as shown:

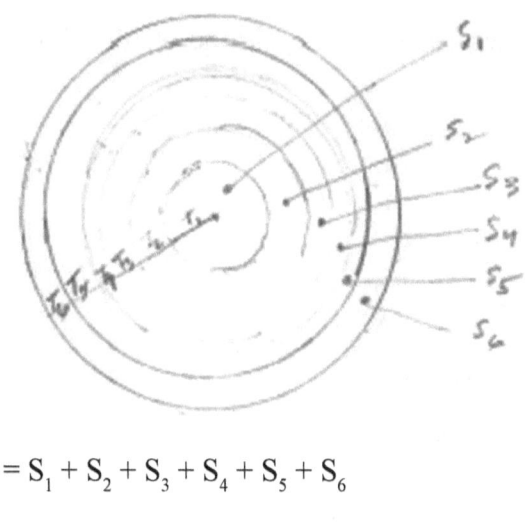

$$A = S_1 + S_2 + S_3 + S_4 + S_5 + S_6$$

$$A = (a+b)^5/(a+b)^4$$

By Nanoizing the area and not the radius we end up with areas of shells, with shell no. 1 being Term 1, shell no. 2 being Term 2. etc.

Shell's Area	Terms	Term #	Value Area
S_1	$a^5/(a+b)^4$	1	.0512
S_2	$5a^4 b/(a+b)^4$	2	.384
S_3	$10 a^3 b^2/(a+b)^4$	3	1.152
S_4	$10 a^2 b^3/(a+b)^4$	4	1.728
S_5	$5 a b^4/(a+b)^4$	5	1.296
S_6	b^5	6	+ .3888
A			5.000

The thickness or width (T_i) is the result of the following computations:

$$S_1 = \pi r^2$$
$$T_1 = (S_1/\pi)^{.5}$$
$$T_1 = (.0512/\pi)^{.5}$$
$$T_1 = .1276615297$$

$$S_1 + S_2 = \pi(T_1 + T_2)^2$$

$$(T_1 + T_2)^2 = \frac{S_1 + S_2}{\pi}$$

$$T_1 + T_2 = \left(\frac{S_1 + S_2}{\pi}\right)^{.5}$$

$$T_2 = \left(\frac{S_1 + S_2}{\pi}\right)^{.5} - T_1$$

$$T_2 = .2445325896$$

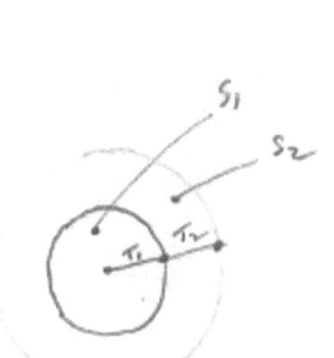

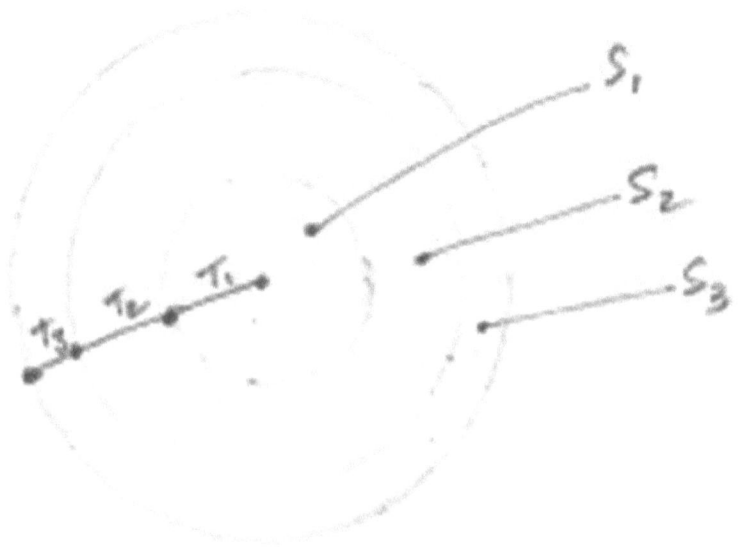

$$S_1 + S_2 + S_3 = \pi(T_1 + T_2 + T_3)^2$$

$$T_1 + T_2 + T_3 = \left[\frac{S_1 + S_2 + S_3}{\pi}\right]^{.5}$$

$$T_3 = \left[\frac{S_1 + S_2 + S_3}{\pi}\right]^{.5} - \left(T_1 + T_2\right)$$

$$T_3 = \left[\frac{1.5872}{\pi}\right]^{.5} - \left(.3721941193\right)$$

$$T_3 = .7107893157 - (.3721941193)$$

$$T_3 = .3385951964$$

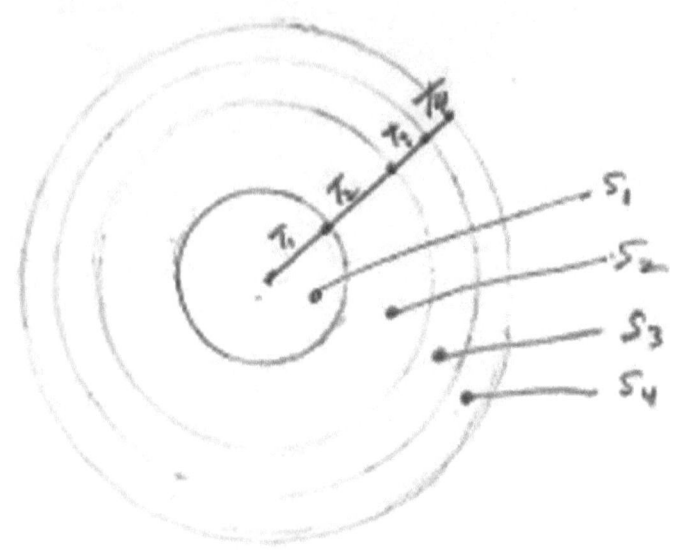

$$S_1 + S_2 + S_3 + S_4 = \pi(T_1 + T_2 + T_3 + T_4)^2$$

$$T_1 + T_2 + T_3 + T_4 = \left[\frac{S_1 + S_2 + S_3 + S_4}{\pi}\right]^{.5}$$

$$T_4 = \left[\frac{S_1 + S_2 + S_3 + S_4}{\pi}\right]^{.5} - \left(T_1 + T_2 + T_3\right)$$

$$T_4 = \left(\frac{3.3152}{\pi}\right)^{.5} - \left(.7107893157\right)$$

$$T_4 = .3164696267$$

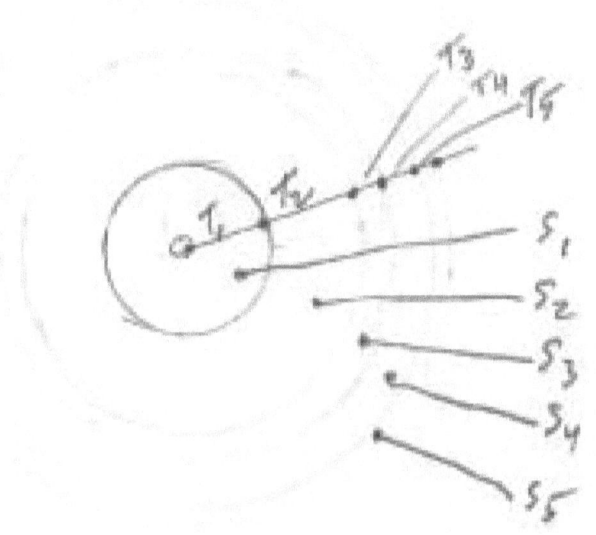

$$S_1 + S_2 + S_3 + S_4 + S_5 = \pi(T_1 + T_2 + T_3 + T_4 + T_5)^2$$

$$T_1 + T_2 + T_3 + T_4 + T_5 = \left(\frac{S_1 + S_2 + S_3 + S_4 + S_5}{\pi}\right)^{.5}$$

$$T_5 = \left[\frac{S_1 + S_2 + S_3 + S_4 + S_5}{\pi}\right]^{.5} - \left(T_1 + T_2 + T_3 + T_4\right)$$

$$T_5 = \left[\frac{4.6112}{\pi}\right]^{.5} - \left(1.027258942\right)$$

$$T_5 = .1842651173$$

$$S_1 + S_2 + S_3 + S_4 + S_5 + S_6 = \pi \left(T_1 + T_2 + T_3 + T_4 + T_5 + T_6\right)^2$$

$$T_1 + T_2 + T_3 + T_4 + T_5 + T_6 = \left(\frac{S_1 + S_2 + S_3 + S_4 + S_5 + S_6}{\pi}\right)^{.5}$$

$$T_6 = \left[\frac{S_1 + S_2 + S_3 + S_4 + S_5 + S_6}{\pi}\right]^{.5} - \left(T_1 + T_2 + T_3 + T_4 + T_5\right)$$

$$T_6 = \left(\frac{5}{\pi}\right)^{.5} - \left(1.209910115\right)$$

$$T_6 = .0515656146$$

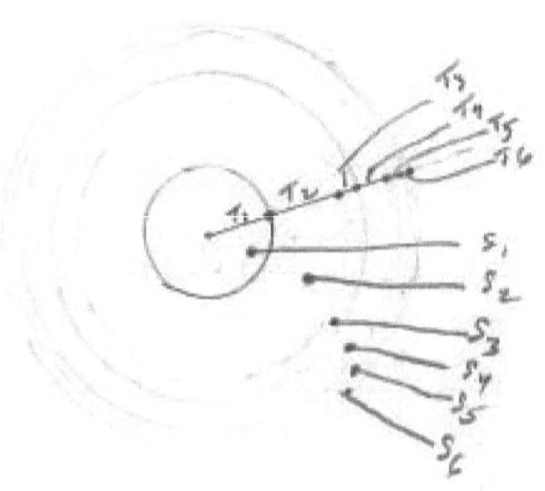

$$R = (A/\pi)^{.5} = 1.261566261$$

$$R = T_1 + T_2 + T_3 + T_4 + T_5 + T_6$$
$$= 1.263180206$$

5) A Binomial Base Triangle: T

B = base, B = a+b, A = ½ Bh, a = 2, b = 3, h = 10, A = 25

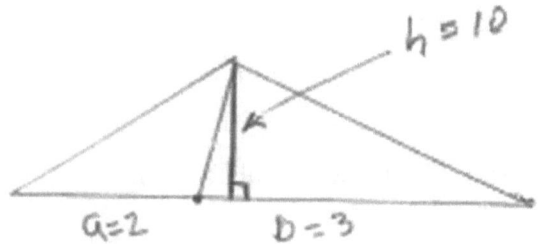

Nanoize the base from
a+b to $B_1 + B_2 + B_3 + B_4 + B_5$

Produce:
Vertical Foil with Nanomial Theorem
Label appropriate headings on Table - Base, Terms, Term #,
Value - Area
Under each label fill in corresponding info.
    For example:

Base	Terms	Term #	Value	Nano-Area
B_1	$a^4/(a+b)^3$	1	.128 (10)(½)	= .64
B_2	$a^3/(a+b)^3$	2	¦	¦
¦	¦	¦	¦	¦
¦	¦	¦	¦	¦

Solution next page.

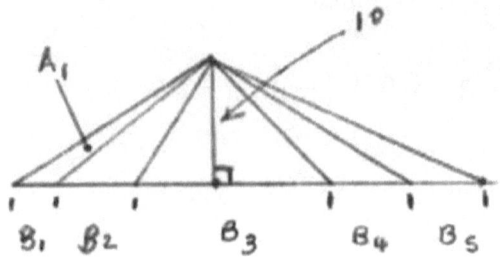

Nanomial Vertical Table/Nanomial Theorem

Base	Terms	Term #	Value		Nano-Area
B_1	$a^4/(a+b)^3$	1	.128 (½)(10)	=	.64
B_2	$4\,a^3\,b/(a+b)^3$	2	.768 (½)(10)	=	.384
B_3	$6\,a^2\,b^2/(a+b)^3$	3	1.728 (½)(10)	=	8.64
B_4	$4\,a\,b^3/(a+b)^3$	4	1.728 (½)(10)	=	8.64
$\underline{B_5}$	$b^4/(a+b)^3$	5	$\underline{+\ 6.48\ (½)(10)}$	+ =	$\underline{3.24}$
B			5		A = 25

$$A = ½(B_1 + B_2 + B_3 + B_4 + B_5)(10)$$

$$= 25$$

6) A plane square: Q

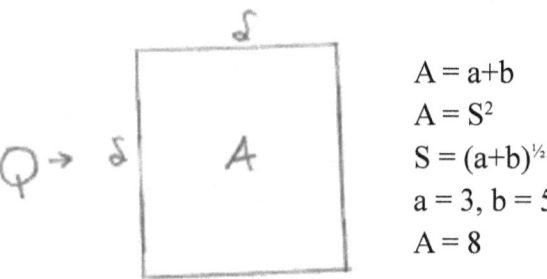

$A = a+b$
$A = S^2$
$S = (a+b)^{1/2}$
$a = 3, b = 5$
$A = 8$

Nanoize Q to four square shells.
example:
$A = a+b$ $\qquad$ $A = (a+b)^3/(a+b)^2$

Area	Terms	Term #	Value
A_1	$a^3/(a+b)^2$	1	.421875
A_2	$3\,a^2\,b/(a+b)^2$	2	2.109375
A_3	$3\,a\,b^2/(a+b)^2$	3	3.515625
A_4	$b^3/(a+b)^2$	4	1.953125
$A =$			8

The next page shows a downward view of a square pyramid.

Here is the elevation view.

$S_1 = .6495190528$

$S_2 = 1.590990258$

$S_3 = 2.459039447$

$S_4 = 2.828427125$

T = Thickness of shells

$T_1 + T_2 + T_3 + T_4 = \frac{1}{2}S$

$T_1 = \frac{1}{2}S_1 = .3247596264$

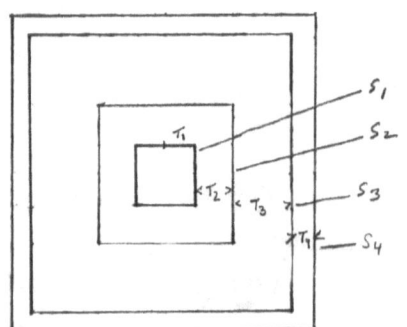

$T_2 = \frac{1}{2}(S_2 - S_1) = .4707356026$

$T_3 = \frac{1}{2}(S_3 - S_2) = .4340245945$

$T_4 = \frac{1}{2}(S_4 - S_3) = .184693839$

T = 1.414213663
check:

    S = 2T
      = 2.828427325
    also:

    $S = \sqrt{a+b}$
      $= \sqrt{8}$
      = 2.828427125

A Sphere: S

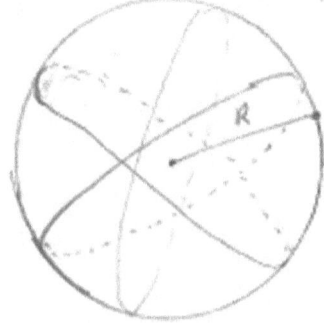

$$V_S = a+b$$

$$V_S = \frac{4}{3} \pi R^3;$$

$$a = 2, b = 4,$$

$$V_S = 6$$

$$R = \left(\frac{3(6)}{4\pi} \right)^{\frac{1}{3}}$$

$$R = \left(\frac{4.5}{\pi} \right)^{\frac{1}{3}}$$

$$R = 1.127251652$$

$$T_i = \text{thickness of shell}$$

Nanoize to four Spherical Shells:

$$V = (a+b)$$
$$V = (a+b)^3/(a+b)^2$$

Vol	Terms	Term #	Value		Thickness Shell
V_1	$a^3/(a+b)^2$	1	$.\overline{2}$	?	.3757505506
V_2	$3\,a^2\,b/(a+b)^2$	2	$1.\overline{3}$	?	.3560017772
V_3	$3\,a\,b^2/(a+b)^2$	3	$2.\overline{6}$	?	.2709010609
V_4	$b^3/(a+b)^2$	4	$1.\overline{7}$	?	.1245982631

R_1 = radius of core
= T_1

$$V_1 = \frac{4}{3}\pi R_1^3$$

$$R_1 = \left(\frac{3V_1}{4\pi}\right)^{\frac{1}{3}}$$

$$T_1 = R_1 = .3757505506$$

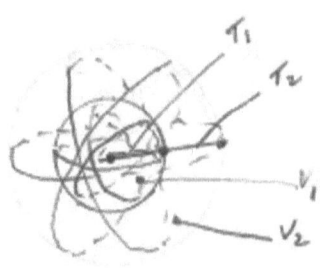

$$R_2 = T_1 + T_2$$

$$T_2 = R_2 - T_1$$

$$T_2 = .3560017772$$

$$V_1 + V_2 = \frac{4}{3}\pi R_2^3$$

$$R_2 = \left[\frac{3(V_1 + V_2)}{4\pi}\right]^{\frac{1}{3}}$$

$$R_2 = \left[\frac{3(.\overline{2} + 1.\overline{3})}{4\pi}\right]^{\frac{1}{3}}$$

$$R_2 = .7187849451$$

$$V_3 = 2.\overline{6}$$

$$R_3 = T_1 + T_2 + T_3$$

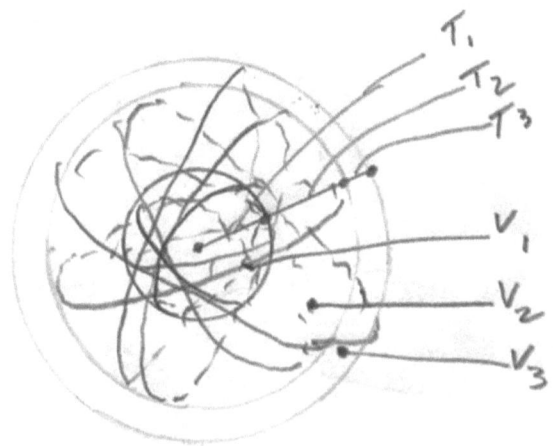

$$V_1 + V_2 + V_3 = \frac{4}{3}\pi R_3{}^3$$

$$V_1 + V_2 + V_3 = \frac{4}{3}\pi (T_1 + T_2 + T_3)^3$$

$$T_3 = \left[\frac{3(V_1 + V_2 + V_3)}{4\pi}\right]^{\frac{1}{3}} - (T_1 + T_2)$$

$$T_3 = .2709010609$$

$V_4 = 1.\overline{7}$

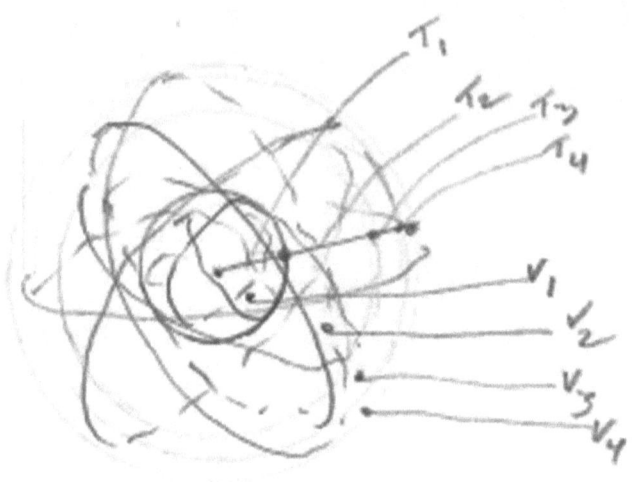

$$6 = \frac{4}{3}\pi\,(T_1 + T_2 + T_3 + T_4)^3$$

$$T_1 + T_2 + T_3 + T_4 = \left(\frac{4.5}{\pi}\right)^{\frac{1}{3}}$$

$$T_4 = \left(\frac{4.5}{\pi}\right)^{\frac{1}{3}} - \left(T_1 + T_2 + T_3\right)$$

$T_4 = .1245982631$

$R_4 = T_1 + T_2 + T_3 + T_4 = 1.127251652$

$$\text{check:}\ V_S = \frac{4}{3}\pi\,(T_1 + T_2 + T_3 + T_4)^3$$

$$= 6$$

A Cube: D

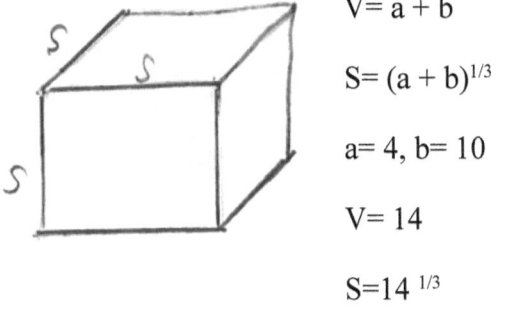

$V = a + b$

$S = (a + b)^{1/3}$

$a = 4, b = 10$

$V = 14$

$S = 14^{1/3}$

$= 2.410142264$

Nanoize to four shells:

$V = a + b$

$V = (a + b)^3 / (a + b)^2$

Vol	Terms	Term#	Value
V_1	$a^3 / (a + b)^2$	1	.3265306122
V_2	$3a^2b / (a + b)^2$	2	2.448979592
V_3	$3ab^2 / (a + b)^2$	3	6.12244898
V_4	$b^3 / (a + b)^2$	4	<u>5.102040816</u>
V			14

For thicknesses of the shells, see next page.

T_1, T_2, T_3, + T_4 are shells' thickness.

$V_1 = .3265306122$

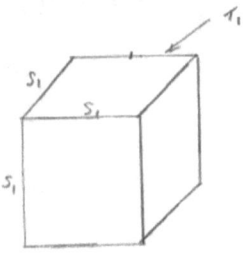

$$S_1 = (.3265306122)^{\frac{1}{3}}$$

$$S_1 = .6886120762$$
$$T_1 = S_{\frac{1}{2}} = .3443060381$$

$V_2 = 2.448979592$

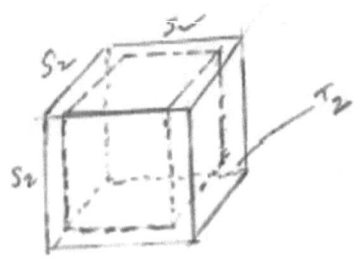

$$S_2 = (V_1 + V_2)^{\frac{1}{3}}$$

$$S_2 = (2.775510204)^{\frac{1}{3}}$$

$$S_2 = 1.405338496$$
$$T_2 = (S_2 - S_1)/2 = .3583632099$$

$V_3 = 6.12244898$

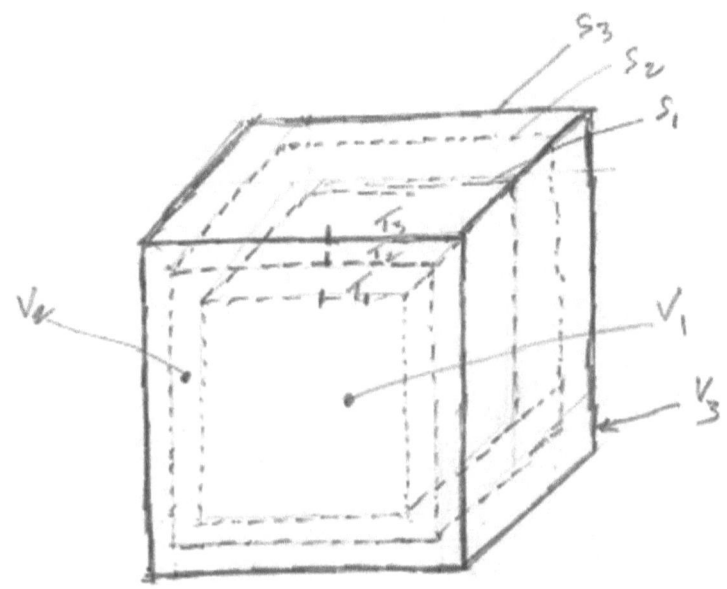

$$S_3 = (V_1 + V_2 + V_3)^{\frac{1}{3}}$$

$$S_3 = (8.897959184)^{\frac{1}{3}}$$

$$S_3 = 2.072192686$$

$$T_3 = \text{Thickness} = (S_3 - S_2)/2$$

$$= .3334278949$$

$V_4 = 5.102040816$

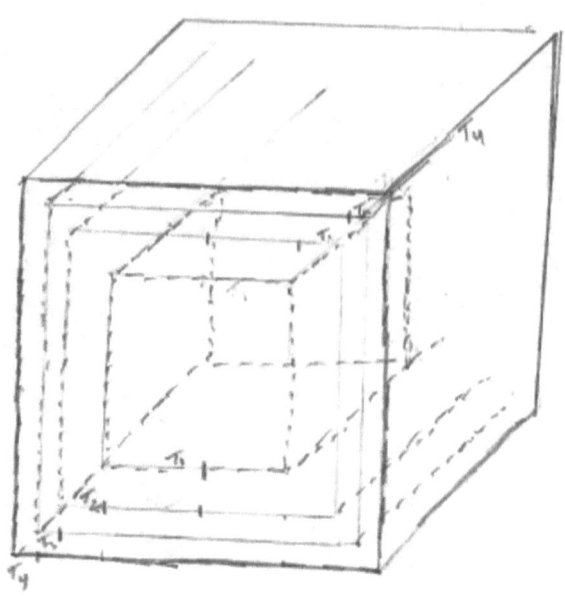

$$S_4 = (V_1 + V_2 + V_3 + V_4)^{\frac{1}{3}}$$

$$S_4 = 2.410142264$$

$$T_4 = (S_4 - S_3)/2$$

$$T_4 = .168974789$$

$$2T_1 + 2T_2 + 2T_3 + 2T_4 = 2.410043862$$

check:

$$V_D = (2.410043862)^3$$
$$= 13.99828528$$

A Cone: P

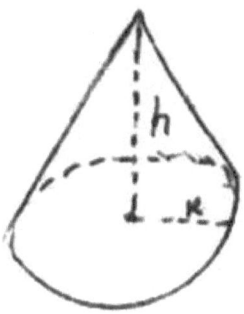

$V_p = a+b,$ $a = 2, b = 3, V = 5$

$V_p = \dfrac{1}{3} h\pi R^2,$ $R = \left(\dfrac{15}{10\pi}\right)^{\frac{1}{2}}$

$h = 10$ $R = .6909882989$

Nanoize Cone 'P' to 4 cone shells

$$V_p = (a+b)^3/(a+b)^2$$
$$V_p = V_1 + V_2 + V_3 + V_4$$

Shell	Terms	Term #	Value
V_1	$a^3/(a+b)^2$	1	.32
V_2	$3\,a^2\,b/(a+b)^2$	2	1.44
V_3	$3\,a\,b^2/(a+b)^2$	3	2.16
V_4	$b^3/(a+b)^2$	4	1.08
$V_p =$			5

$V_1 = .32$

$V_1 = \dfrac{\pi h}{3} T_1^2$

$T_1^2 = \dfrac{3V_1}{\pi h}$

$T_1 = \left[\dfrac{3V_1}{\pi h} \right]^{.5} = \frac{1}{2}$ radius

$T_1 = .1748077489$
cone shell$_1 = V_1$

$V_2 = 1.44$

$V_1 + V_2 = \dfrac{\pi h}{3}(T_1 + T_2)^2$

$T_2 = \left[\dfrac{3(V_1 + V_2)}{\pi h} \right]^{1/2} - T_1$

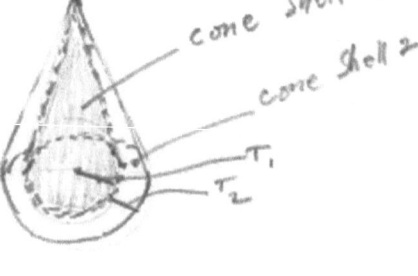

$T_2 = .235152761$

cone shell$_2 = V_2$

    If cone C_1 is removed from cone C_2, then cone shell C_2 is left. Cone Shell$_2 = V_2$

$V_3 = 2.16$

$$V_1 + V_2 + V_3 = \frac{\pi h}{3}\left(T_1 + T_2 + T_3\right)^2$$

$$T_1 + T_2 + T_3 = \left[\frac{3\left(V_1 + V_2 + V_3\right)}{\pi h}\right]^{.5}$$

$$T_3 = \left[\frac{3\left(V_1 + V_2 + V_3\right)}{\pi h}\right]^{.5} - \left(T_1 + T_2\right)$$

$T_3 = .201866612$

cone shell$_3$ = V_3

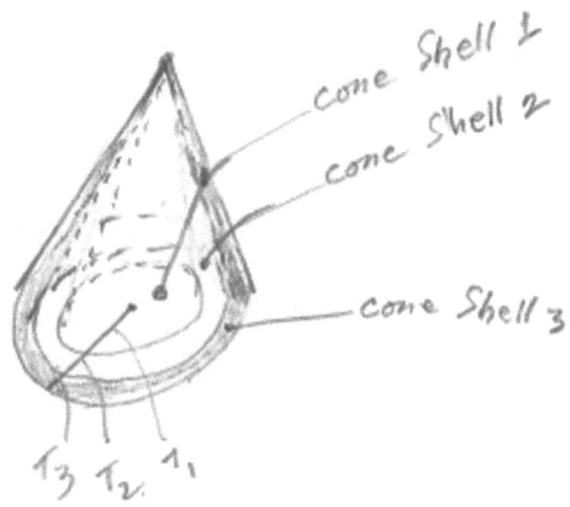

If cone shell$_1$ and cone shell$_2$ are removed from cone$_3$, then cone shell$_3$ is left.

$V_4 = 1.08$

$$V_1 + V_2 + V_3 + V_4 = \frac{\pi h}{3}\left(T_1 + T_2 + T_3 + T_4\right)^2$$

$$T_1 + T_2 + T_3 + T_4 = \left[\frac{3\left(V_1 + V_2 + V_3 + V_4\right)}{\pi h}\right]^{.5}$$

$$T_4 = \left[\frac{3\left(V_1 + V_2 + V_3 + V_4\right)}{\pi h}\right]^{.5} - \left(T_1 + T_2 + T_3\right)$$

$T_4 = .079161177$

Check: $R = T_1 + T_2 + T_3 + T_4$
$R = .6909882989$

cone shell$_4$ = V_4

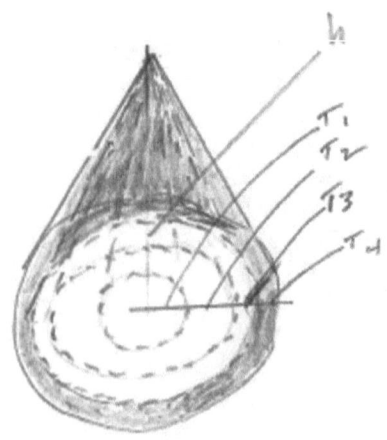

If cone shell$_1$, cone shell$_2$, and cone shell$_3$ are removed from cone$_4$ then, cone shell$_4$ is left.

A Binomial Area Triangle: Z

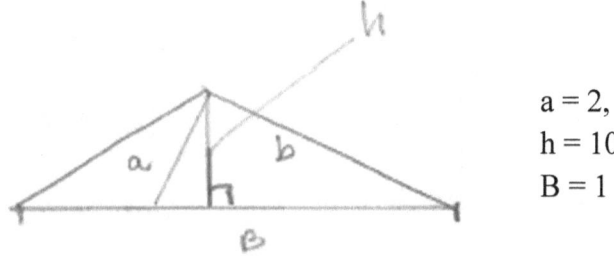

$a = 2, b = 3$
$h = 10$
$B = 1$

$A = \frac{1}{2} B h$, $A = a+b$, $A = (a+b)^4/(a+b)^3$

Nanoize Triangle. Z's area (A)
Find: Nano bases and areas

Area	Terms	Term #1	Value	Base
A_1	$a^4/(a+b)^3$	1	.128	.0256
A_2	$4\,a^3\,b/(a+b)^3$	2	.768	.1536
A_3	$6\,a^2\,b^2/(a+b)^3$	3	1.728	.3456
A_4	$4\,ab^3/(a+b)^3$	4	1.728	.3456
A_5	$b^4/(a+b)^3$	5	.648	.1296
$A =$			5	1

check: A = 5 (given)

$A = \frac{1}{2} h B$
$A = \frac{1}{2} (10) (1)$
$A = 5$

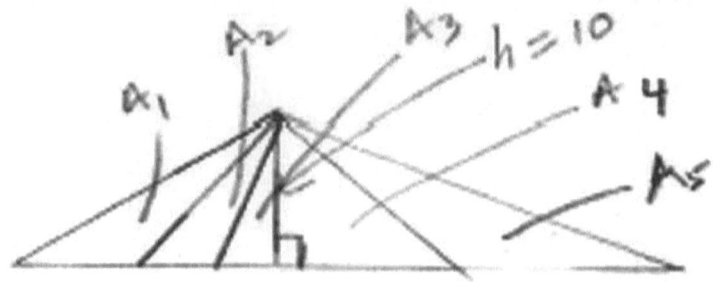

In this example the area was nanoized from a+b (two pieces) to $A_1 + A_2 + A_3 + A_4 + A_5$ (Five pieces).

In the other Triangle example. Triangle 'T', the base was nanoized from a+b (Two pieces) to $B_1 + B_2 + B_3 + B_4 + B_5$ (five pieces).

Another important concept: when

a cube's vol is nanoized, Solid shells will be produced,

if sides of a cube are nanoized then, small rectangular solids will be produced as a result of the sides being nanoized;

if sides of a square are nanoized, then smaller rectangles will be produced as of a result of the sides being nanoized;

if area of a square is nanoized then shell areas will be produced.

If Job 'B' takes 7 seconds to complete, and can be separated into 2' pieces, a+b and represented:

Job 'B →

a	b
2	5

a+b = 7

a = 2, b = 5

Nanoize this Job into 7 pieces.

$(a+b)^6/(a+b)^5$

Job	Terms	Term #	Value
$J_1(sec)$	$a^6/(a+b)^5$	1	.0038079372
J_2	$6\,a^5\,b/(a+b)^5$	2	.0571190575
J_3	$15\,a^4\,b^2/(a+b)^5$	3	.3569941096
J_4	$20\,a^3\,b^3/(a+b)^5$	4	1.189980365
J_5	$15\,a^2\,b^4/(a+b)^5$	5	2.231213185
J_6	$6\,a\,b^5/(a+b)^5$	6	2.231213185
$+\,J_7$	$b^6/(a+b)^5$	7	+ .9296721604
$J =$			7

Job 'B'

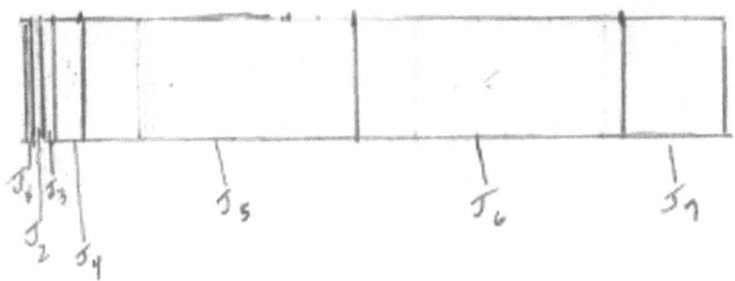

Not to scale.

So, from looking at J = a+b we see that Job part 'a' can be done in 2 sec and Job part 'b' in 5 sec.

If we nanoize Job 'B' from 2 parts to 7 parts, J_1, J_2, J_3, J_4, J_5, J_6 & J_7, shown on Job Table, show values for each part.

By using Nanoization, predetermined term values are a result. This is very important, imagine several Jobs working together or one after another, or in combinations, Total Jobs will be predetermined to finish on time!

As you can see, with a little imagination, all the different ways the sciences will be changed.

Nanomial's going to have a great future.

CHAPTER V

It seems like fifty years just flew by, but I look back at all the trials and errors of development; it seems so long ago, when I first heard "binomial."

Little did I know how all this would turn out. But, now I know that 'Binomial's relative has always been there. Nanomial was so illusive. I gave up at times, but somehow, I knew Nanomial was close by, I just happened to meet Nanomial before anyone else did. I had fun and disappointments.

Before closing, I would like to say, Binomial has other relatives, care to guess?

They are high tech individuals, but they are still part of Nanomial, I met them and so have you. I wanted to mix ( )'s with them. They said, "we don't have time, and they wanted to know "what are ( ) removals?".

Maybe, you would like to meet Namomial's children The oldest one is Squarnano, then, Rectanglnano, then Shellnano. I'm introducing them in the order that they came to me, developed from 'Salcido's Vertical Nanomial Foils' and Salcido's Nanomial Theorem. These nanos have dimensions not, ( )'s.

The dimensions could be considered to be their IDs, finger prints, gps locations, etc. And, within these nomials, information may be stored.

The information could be DNA instruction, bar code, arrays of arrays of all information needed via addresses. Squarnano and Rectanglnano could be processed in a physical, chemical, or radio-wave transfer; Shellnano could be used for design.

These blocks or cubes of information on DNA instruction sets may be sent ahead in a radial or linear direction to a specific or unknown locations that will be in its path, to see if life is sustainable. For example, the DNA information for an apple (digital or analog) would trigger the process of life if the ingrediants were present to produce an apple (life), similar to planting a seed.

Well, I'll leave that for someone else's 50 years.

Shellnano is a shell derivative of a plane or solid, another way to look at shellnano - blankets of different thicknesses on top of each other around a plane or solid core.

Hopefully the least this book has

accomplished is, that you may now expand a binomial of any real power with hardly any trouble.

www.ingramcontent.com/pod-product-compliance
Lightning Source LLC
Chambersburg PA
CBHW021247280526
45784CB00005B/2267